INDIAN JEWELRY
of the
Prehistoric Southwest

Superb examples of prehistoric overlay work, with the Superstition Mountains of Arizona in the background.

INDIAN JEWELRY
of the
Prehistoric Southwest

photographs by
JERRY D. JACKA
text by
NANCY S. HAMMACK

THE UNIVERSITY OF ARIZONA PRESS
Tucson, Arizona

The prehistoric Indian utilized the variety of raw materials available to him. Foreground: argillite beads. Left to right: jet beads with turquoise pendant, polished pebbles with bone and shell disc beads, whole Conus shells and shell disc beads, mudstone and shell beads, turquoise and jet beads.

THE UNIVERSITY OF ARIZONA PRESS

I.S.B.N.-0-8165-0515-2
L.C. No. 75-8017

Man, from the earliest times, has considered the adornment of his person to be as necessary as food and shelter. The Indians of the Southwestern United States are no exception. They have loved fine jewelry, esteemed it as wealth, and worn it profusely. Today the use of Indian jewelry has spread far beyond its original boundaries and its appreciation has become world-wide.

The Indians' traditional appreciation of beautiful jewelry was recorded by the earliest Spanish explorers and missionaries. As they came into the Southwest, they reported being met by people wearing feather headdresses, strings of beads, bracelets, and ear pendants. In 1539, the Spanish missionary Fray Marcos de Niza wrote of "the number of turquoises worn as ornaments by the people. Some had as many as three or four strings of green stones around their neck; others carried them as earpendants and in their noses." These people were the ancestors of the present Southwestern Indians, and were the descendants of those who created and wore the jewelry excavated today from prehistoric ruins.

The prehistoric cultures of the Southwest—those prior to Spanish contacts, about 1500 A.D.—generally are divided into three main groups: Hohokam, Mogollon, and Anasazi. Among all three were found agriculture, irrigation, pottery, baskets, weaving, and stone and shell jewelry. Each group, with its distinctive traits and traditions, occupied a definable geographic area. But these boundaries expanded or shrank due to such things as abundant crops or crop failures, depletion of natural resources, internal conflicts, and natural phenomena. As a result, various subcultures came into being.

Rendered by Doug Mellis, State Museum, University of Arizona.

Painting of a Hohokam man arrayed in a bone hairpin, turquoise earrings, argillite cheek plugs hung with parrot or macaw feathers, a nose plug inset with turquoise, a turquoise and argillite mosaic overlay pendant, a Glycymeris shell bracelet, an argillite bracelet, and two shell rings. Body painting completes this portrayal.

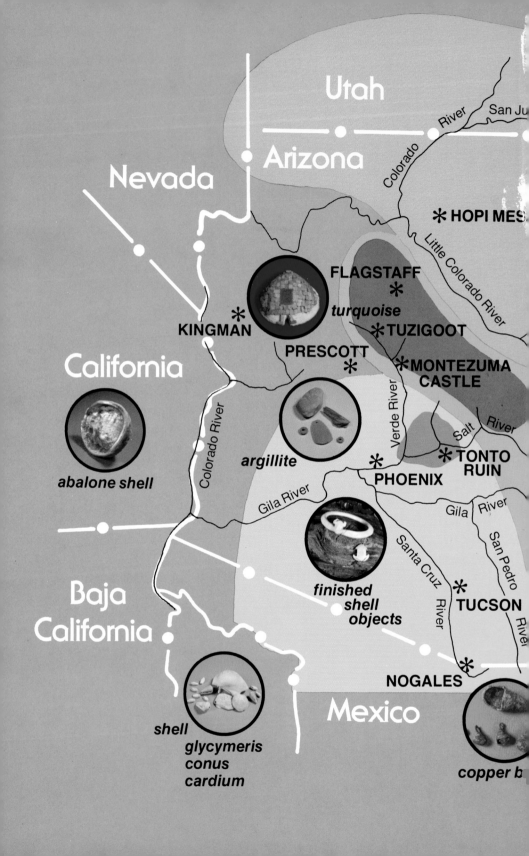

Utah

Nevada

Arizona

Colorado River

San Ju

*HOPI MES

Little Colorado River

FLAGSTAFF
*

*KINGMAN

turquoise

*TUZIGOOT

PRESCOTT
*

*MONTEZUMA
CASTLE

California

Verde River

Salt River

abalone shell

argillite

*TONTO
RUIN

*
PHOENIX

Colorado River

Gila River

Gila River

finished
shell
objects

Santa Cruz River

San Pedro River

*
TUCSON

Baja
California

NOGALES
*

Mexico

copper b

shell
glycymeris
conus
cardium

Colorado

MESA VERDE
*

River

CHACO *
CANYON
jet

* **GALLUP**

* **ZUNI**

ALBUQUERQUE
*

turquoise

Rio Grande River

New Mexico

Mimbres River

* **EL PASO**

Texas

Culture Areas
☐ ANASAZI
☐ HOHOKAM
☐ MOGOLLON
☐ SALADO
☐ SINAGUA

Sources of raw materials used by the prehistoric Indian cultures of the Southwest to create their magnificent jewelry.

The people that Fray Marcos de Niza described were the Pimas, who since Spanish contact have lived near what is now Phoenix, Arizona, and are the descendants of the ancient Hohokam. The Hohokam probably migrated north from Mexico about 300 B.C. and settled in the Gila and Salt river valleys, where they intensively cultivated the surrounding desert by means of hundreds of miles of hand-dug canals. Although their dwellings were only scattered flimsy brush shelters, they eventually built elaborate ball courts and platform mounds for religious ceremonies. The Hohokam cremated their dead with many offerings, burying the ashes in their typical red-on-buff pottery vessels.

When the Hohokam arrived from Mexico they were already making beautiful shell jewelry. Throughout their history they refined and elaborated upon this art, trading the products to their neighbors, the Mogollon and Anasazi.

Tiny Hohokam carved shell pendant of a man standing on a lizard. The figure itself is only one inch high.

Abalone shell, with three pre-historic abalone pendants.

The dime on which this Hohokam stone duck is sitting emphasizes its minute size.

Mimbres jewelry, with examples of the unique Mimbres Black-on-white pottery. The Mimbres culture developed from the Mogollon in southwestern New Mexico during the thirteenth century.

Concurrent with the arrival of the Hohokam in the Southwest, the Mogollon culture was developing in the high lands of east-central Arizona and southwestern New Mexico, where hunting and gathering peoples were learning to make pottery and cultivate crops from their Mexican neighbors. Throughout most of their history the Mogollon lived in timber lodges dug into the earth, all located around a central ceremonial structure. Their jewelry can best be characterized by simplicity, the most abundant forms being disc beads and pendants of shell and stone, and thin *Glycymeris* shell bracelets.

A magnificent Mogollon necklace of disc and bi-lobed shell beads with a Conus *shell pendant.*

Mogollon shell jewelry. Top left: *shell disc beads*. Top right: Olivella *shell beads*. Bottom, left to right: *shell ring*, Conus *shells, thin* Glycymeris *shell bracelet, small bi-valve shells strung as beads*.

Anasazi jet and shell disc beads, turquoise pendants and earrings, and small stone and turquoise figures.

Agriculture and pottery-making soon spread from the Mogollon northward to the Anasazi Basketmakers in the four corners area of Utah, Arizona, Colorado, and New Mexico. By 900 A.D. their culture was in full flower, distinguished by large communal masonry dwellings, ruins of which still exist at Chaco Canyon and Mesa Verde. They had sufficient leisure time to produce exquisite jewelry and beautiful black-on-white pottery. Their favorite materials for jewelry were turquoise and jet, both locally mined. In the twelfth century drought caused most of the Anasazi areas to be abandoned. The people then concentrated on the Hopi Mesas in northern Arizona, along the Rio Grande River, and in the Zuni and Acoma areas of New Mexico, where they still carry on the tradition of fine jewelry making.

*A variety of Anasazi beads with an early Hopi Jeddito
Black-on-yellow jar.*

After the eruption of Sunset Crater near Flagstaff, Arizona, in 1065 A.D., the surrounding soil was left very fertile. People from neighboring cultures then moved into the area and the intermingling resulted in the Sinagua culture. They built multi-roomed masonry houses and ceremonial ball courts, and fabricated an extensive variety of jewelry.

Typical Sinagua jewelry and stone axes.

*A pottery jar draped with Sinagua jewelry excavated
from Tuzigoot Ruin, in the Verde Valley, Arizona.*

The many varieties of necklaces found in Sinagua ruins, displayed in front of Montezuma Castle in central Arizona.

An overlay pendant on a string of shell beads and turquoise chunks.
The Salado homeland provides the desert background.

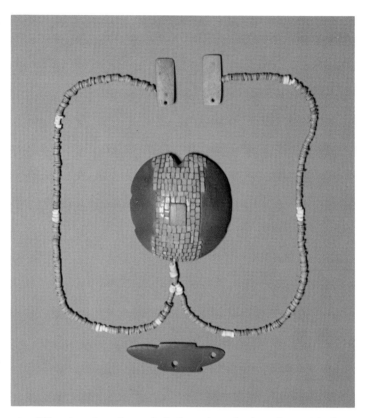

Argillite jewelry from Salado ruins dating from 1150 to 1400 A.D. The pendant is inlaid with turquoise.

Cross of turquoise mosaic on wood backing, found at the Lower Tonto Cliff Dwelling, Tonto National Monument, Arizona.

Unusual flower or sunburst earrings of shell and turquoise from the Tonto Basin, Arizona.

Like the Sinagua, the Salado culture was a blending of diverse traits from surrounding Hohokam, Mogollon, and Anasazi groups. Around 1100 A.D., in the Tonto Basin and the higher foothills to the north in Arizona, the Salado began making their distinctive red, black, and white pottery, and began building complex masonry structures enclosed within compound walls. The workmanship of their jewelry, particularly the overlay pieces, is unsurpassed among prehistoric peoples.

Excavating the remains of these prehistoric cultures, archaeologists have discovered evidences of extensive contact and trade among them. Many raw materials and even finished products can be traced back to their original sources. It is easy to envision a meeting between two prehistoric traders on an isolated foot trail. The one, an Anasazi from northwestern New Mexico, is carrying several small black-on-white bowls and a quantity of turquoise. The Hohokam from central Arizona has worked shell in the form of necklaces, bracelets, and pendants, all packed in raw cotton which could be spun and woven into cloth. Using signs, as they probably did not speak the same language, they bartered their wares. They then departed for their homelands, satisfied with their transactions. Early twentieth century Indians could still recall making similar trading expeditions to Mexico in order to exchange turquoise for shells and parrot feathers.

Shell from the Gulf of California and the Pacific coast was the most widely traded single item of jewelry, in both its raw and finished forms. *Cardium* shells were discovered in the early levels of Ventana Cave in southern Arizona. While these probably were used as containers rather than as personal adornment, they indicate contact with the Gulf of California as early as 10,000 years ago. When the Hohokam settled in Arizona, they immediately began making organized shell-collecting expeditions to the Gulf of California. Campsites discovered on these shell routes were found to be strewn with debris left from cutting out crude shell bracelets. In the Hohokam villages along the Gila and Salt rivers, many different types of shell were skillfully worked into fine jewelry, then bartered to neighboring cultures. Very early Anasazi caves in southern Colorado have yielded

Examples of fine Hohokam shell work.

Olivella and *Conus* shell beads, worked shell disc beads, and shell pendants. *Glycymeris* shell bracelets and shell beads have been found in the early Anasazi sites of Chaco Canyon, New Mexico. The Mogollon also possessed Hohokam shell jewelry from the beginning of their history. Shells were so prized that imitations often were carved from more common materials.

Turquoise is another material highly prized by the southwestern Indians, both prehistoric and modern. The Anasazi worked many turquoise mines in the area of Cerrillos, southeast of Santa Fe, New Mexico. Cerrillos turquoise, which is noted for its color, has been found in prehistoric sites far south in Mexico. The Hohokam had access to many mines in Arizona, among them Bisbee and Kingman. One of their favorite uses of the blue gem was to incorporate it into overlay, although they also made it into pendants, beads, and earrings.

Salado and Hohokam pendants and a late Anasazi bone hairpin with extremely fine turquoise overlay.

Finely carved frog of jet or lignite, strung on turquoise and jet beads, from the Tonto Basin, Arizona.

In addition to shell and turquoise, an immense variety of other natural materials was fabricated into jewelry. Black lignite, or jet, was mined by the Anasazi from local bituminous coal beds. Easily carved into pendants, finger rings, and beads, it took on a soft luster when polished and was particularly effective in mosaics with turquoise and shell. Red argillite was dug from the hills around Prescott, Arizona, and carved into a variety of forms. Many other nonpermanent adornments, such as body paint and feathers were reported by the early Spanish explorers.

Considering the importance of trade relationships in the Southwest, it is evident that although a raw material such as argillite or turquoise might appear naturally in the area of a particular culture, its use was not confined to that culture, nor was a piece of jewelry necessarily produced where it was found. It might have been made of materials from widely scattered sources with the finished product traded to yet another area. The most obvious example of this is the Hohokam *Glycymeris* shell bracelet, which commonly was worn by peoples of all southwestern prehistoric cultures.

Argillite bracelet, ring and tiny carvings from Anasazi, Salado and Hohokam sites in Arizona.

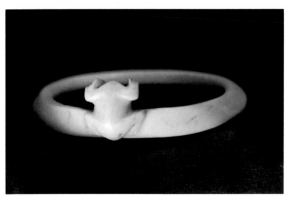

Hohokam Glycymeris *shell bracelet with three dimensional frog carved into the umbo.*

The techniques used to work these materials testify to the great skill and ingenuity of the prehistoric artisans. The Hohokam employed an amazing variety of methods to craft their shell jewelry. Preliminary work was done by grinding, cutting, and drilling. Then the piece might be embellished by carvings or engravings, inlay, overlay (mosaic), painting, or etching. As the tools for this work were limited to sandstones and other native rocks, the time required to complete some of the more delicate and intricate pieces must have been extensive.

Bracelets, cut from the circular outside edge of *Glycymeris* shells, were the most abundant shell ornament produced by the Hohokam. The band portion was often incised (the grooves frequently filled with paint) in geometric or naturalistic designs. The umbo, or thick valve portion, was often carved into a three-dimensional figure—commonly a frog or bird—or covered with overlay work. Shell was also utilized in rings, beads, pendants, and mosaics. Beads were either whole *Olivella* or *Conus* shells or ground disc types. The variety of styles in shell pendants included whole, ground, and cut shells, in geometric and life forms.

Glycymeris *shell bracelets. Two in the foreground*
show unusual mask-like carvings.

Turquoise pendants and earrings, turquoise and shell mosaic pendant, and carved shell pendant, along with a banded green-stone animal effigy and Sacaton Red-on-buff pottery plate, crafted by the Hohokam of the Gila and Salt river valleys, Arizona, between 700 and 1200 A.D.

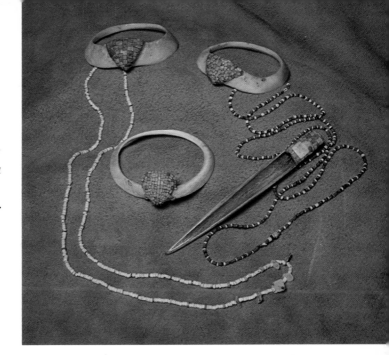

Turquoise overlay technique shown on shell bracelets and a bone hairpin.

Among the most spectacular of all prehistoric jewelry forms were the shells completely covered with mosaic overlay. Small carved pieces of turquoise, argillite, jet, and shell were affixed with a natural gum to the backs of large bivalve shells. Often more perishable materials such as wood or basketry were used as a backing. As both the gum adhesive and backing materials have usually disintegrated through time, these mosaics are seldom found in their original form and often must be reconstructed.

Basketry arm band with turquoise overlay and original pitch adhesive, found in Ceremonial Cave near El Paso, Texas.

Incised and painted Glycymeris *shell bracelet.*

The process of etching shell, developed by the Hohokam, was unique in both the new and old worlds among prehistoric peoples and represents the culmination of shell working. Laboratory experiments, using materials available to the Hohokam, have reproduced the technique. Portions of large *Cardium* shells, usually the interior or concave side, were coated with a gum or pitch. These areas would be the raised or unetched design elements of the final product. Then the shell was dipped into, or filled with, fermented fruit juice from the saguaro cactus. The exposed portion of shell was eaten away by this impure acetic acid, the height of relief obtained depending upon the length of time the shell was exposed to the acid. After the etching was completed, the design often was further embellished by painting the raised portions. Evidence of painting on shells is very elusive, as the paints were composed of ground minerals which eventually rub or wash off.

A horned toad etched on a large Cardium *shell by the Hohokam between 900 and 1100* A.D.

Perhaps the most amazing prehistoric jewelry products are the millions of shell and stone disc beads which are found throughout the Southwest. Some are so tiny that they will fall through the mesh of a window screen, and their holes are so minute that they cannot be strung with the finest household needle. The process of making these beads is illustrated by a cache of bead-making apparatus found buried with a male skeleton in the Mimbres Valley of southwestern New Mexico. With sandstone, thin fragments of bead material were ground to the desired thickness, then scored and broken into squares for each individual bead. A rough disc was formed by breaking the edges. Each one then was drilled—larger beads by stone-tipped drills, smaller ones with a cactus spine. The beads were then tightly strung and worked back and forth on a sandstone slab to produce a uniform roundness. It was a time-consuming, painstaking process. For example, a deposit of more than 15,000 beads, found unstrung in a burial jar excavated in northern Arizona, made a single strand necklace 32 feet long. Archaeologists figure the maker would have averaged 15 minutes a bead for collecting the raw materials, making his tools and crafting the necklace— thereby taking him 480 days, working 8 hours a day.

Thousands of stone and shell beads crafted by the many prehistoric cultures of the Southwest spill from a prehistoric pottery bowl dating around 1350 A.D.

Beads and pendants were drilled with a pump drill like the one shown here. The wood crosspiece is pulled downward, causing the leather thong to unwind and the shank to spin. The pottery disc weight helps the shank to continue spinning until the thong is twisted in the opposite direction, raising the crosspiece back to the upper position. The crosspiece is again pulled down to repeat the spinning action in a reverse direction. With little practice a high speed spinning action is maintained by "pumping" the crosspiece of this ancient tool.

The only evidence of prehistoric metallurgy found in the Southwest is in copper bells which date from 1000 to 1400 A.D. Since these have never been discovered in any particular ceremonial context, it can be assumed that they were used for personal adornment or, as they are in modern times, as anklets in dances. Analysis has revealed that the origin of the metal used for these bells is local to the southwestern United States or northern Mexico, but the exact location of where they were made is unknown. There is no question that they were cast by the lost wax—*cire perdu*—process. This consisted of making an exact model in wax of the object desired, then surrounding the wax model with clay. As molten metal was poured into the top of the clay mold, the wax melted and ran out through a tiny hole in the bottom, and was replaced by the metal. When the metal had cooled, the clay shell was broken away, leaving the finished form.

Typical copper bells which were cast by the lost wax process in northern Mexico and traded to the Hohokam in Arizona.

Bone carved with geometric designs resembling those painted on the black and white pottery of the Anasazi.

Designs used on prehistoric jewelry normally are referred to as either geometric or naturalistic. Geometric designs often appear to be copied from patterns painted on pottery. The most popular motifs were variously arranged triangles combined with dots and parallel lines. Naturalistic designs were mainly confined to animals; plants were seldom depicted. The Hohokam frequently used the frog, because in their desert environment, frogs are associated with water and appear in great numbers after heavy rains. Cranes and pelicans, both waterfowl, also were favored themes. Others were lizards, horned toads, rattlesnakes, mountain sheep, roadrunners, and various other birds. A motif also widely used in Mexico is that of a bird devouring a snake. But regardless of the design used, it was always well executed and pleasing to the eye.

Exquisitely detailed frogs.

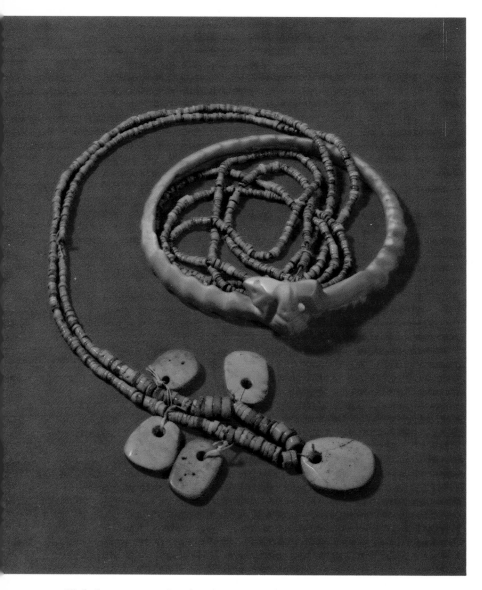

Hohokam turquoise beads and pendants, and a carved Glycymeris *shell bracelet from Snaketown, one of the largest Hohokam sites in Arizona. The carving on the bracelet represents a rattlesnake being held by a bird. The bird's beak is pointing upward and the snake's rattles are to the right of the bird, along the bottom of the bracelet.*

The prehistoric Indians lavished much time and energy upon their jewelry, and the extent of its importance to them is shown by the fact that jewelry has usually been included as grave offerings with both burials and cremations. Southern Colorado caves have yielded desiccated remains of Anasazi basketmakers arrayed in strings of beads, bracelets, earrings and pendants.

Hohokam cremations usually contained at least a few burned beads and often many objects of worked shell. Salado burials were extremely rich, containing particularly intricate overlay items of turquoise and shell. Jewelry, along with tools, food, and clothing, was considered by the prehistoric Indian to be essential to a good life in the afterworld.

The special religious significance that jewelry had can be seen at Chaco Canyon, New Mexico, one of the great Anasazi ceremonial centers. Ceremonial structures were consecrated by deposits of turquoise and necklaces, sealed in niches around the walls. Pueblo Indians consider turquoise to be sacred and scatter chips of it liberally about their shrines. Its blue is one of the sacred colors, a gift from the gods. Turquoise jewelry is an essential element in many Hopi Katchina costumes, and ceremonial dances are made all the more striking by the quantities of turquoise and silver worn by both the participants and spectators. Little imagination is needed to visualize an earlier dance, the figures laden with shell, stone and turquoise beads, earrings, shell bracelets, and copper bells around the ankles.

Whether consciously or subconsciously, the modern Indian jeweler continues in the spirit of his ancestors. He learned silversmithing from the Spanish, thereby expanding his repertoire of materials with a more malleable substance, and enlarging the scope of design. The delicate geometric or curvilinear patterns of Hopi silver overlay still resemble those carved into Hohokam shell bracelets years ago. Santo Domingo turquoise overlay on shell is similar to the workmanship of the ancient Salado. The Zuni craftsmen do particularly magnificent inlay pieces of turquoise, shell, jet, and coral (replacing the red argillite of the prehistoric artisans). They also excel in carving the tiny birds and animals for which their ancestors were noted. Modern beadmakers find it difficult to equal the thinness and delicacy of the earlier ground shell and stone disc beads. By continuing to utilize so many of the local materials of his environment, the modern Indian craftsman shows his closeness to nature, a concern apparent in the many naturalistic elements incorporated into prehistoric jewelry. This continuity of tradition between the old and new is one of the outstanding features of Indian jewelry.

Tiny prehistoric carved stone birds and animals.

Necklace from a Salado burial. The turquoise overlay pieces have been arranged on the pendant in a frog design.

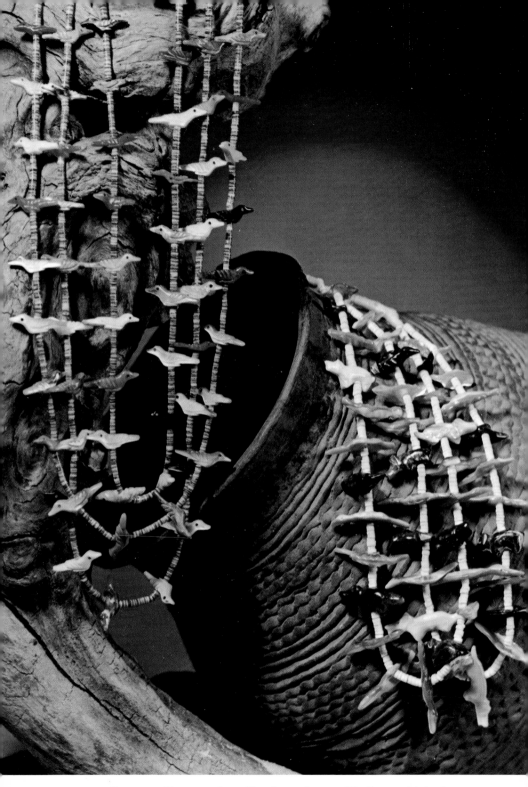

Compare these modern Zuni carvings with the prehistoric ones preceding, noticing the attention to detail in both.